This book belongs to

_____

POETRY
Speaks to Children

EDITOR
Elise Paschen

ILLUSTRATORS
Judy Love
Wendy Rasmussen
Paula Zinngrabe Wendland

SERIES EDITOR
DOMINIQUE RACCAH

ADVISORY EDITORS
Billy Collins
Nikki Giovanni
X. J. Kennedy

SOURCEBOOKS MEDIAFUSION™
AN IMPRINT OF SOURCEBOOKS, INC.®
NAPERVILLE, ILLINOIS

Published by Sourcebooks, Inc. P.O. Box 4410, Naperville, Illinois 60567-4410

phone: (630) 961-3900 fax: (630) 961-2168 www.sourcebooks.com

Library of Congress Cataloging-in-Publication Data

Poetry speaks to children / editor, Elise Paschen.

   p. cm.

 ISBN 1-4022-0329-2 (alk. paper)

 1. Children's poetry, American. 2. Children's poetry, English. I. Paschen, Elise.

PS586.3.P644 2005

811.008'09282—dc22

                      2005023743

Printed and bound in China.

OGP 20 19 18 17 16

Source of Production : O.G. Printing Productions, Ltd. Kowloon, Hong Kong

Date of Production: August 2014

Run Number: 5002138

The Poetry Speaks Tradition

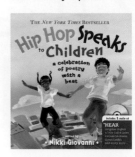

Hip Hop Speaks to Children

$19.99 U.S./$21.99 CAN

The Tree That Time Built

$19.99 U.S./$24.99 CAN

Available in bookstores everywhere.

ABOUT THE CD

This audio CD includes:

- 68 minutes of engaging and enriching poetry on 58 tracks. The Table of Contents shows you the tracks and track numbers, plus each poem with a reading displays the track number on the page.
- 50 poems read by 34 poets and artists. Use the Index at the back to find your favorite poems and poets!
- 29 poets, past and present, reading their own work.
- 27 original recordings—you'll only find them here.
- Plus a few wildcards, just for fun!

We hope you'll listen to the CD while you read the book— or enjoy it all on its own!

Contents

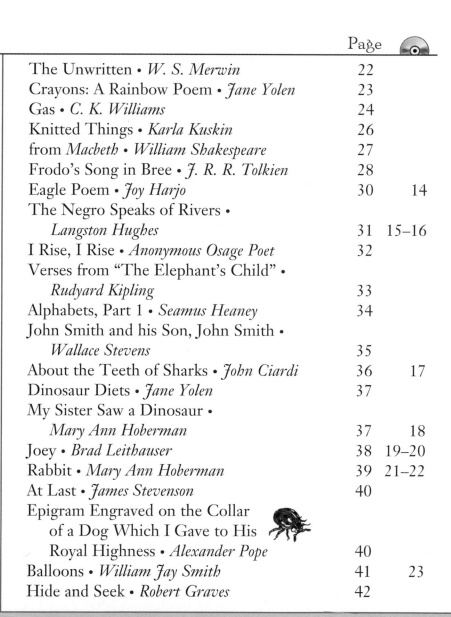

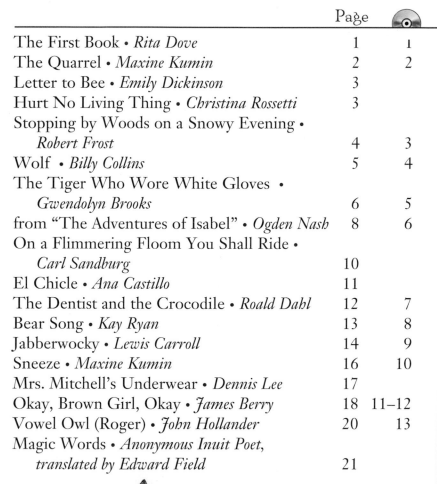

Page

A Note from the publisher

Welcome to *Poetry Speaks to Children*, a completely unique kind of children's poetry book. In the eighteen years that I have been the publisher of Sourcebooks, I will admit to loving this book the most. I hope this is a book you too will come to love. Its format is:

- Strongly visual—a picture book in poetry
- Full of storytelling—a storybook in poetry
- Packed with sound, taking advantage of the wonderful range of voices that makes poetry a performance art
- Ageless—a book that can grow with a child and be loved by an adult
- Filled with the classic poetry of your childhood and the great new voices of today's poets

Poetry Speaks to Children (like its parent, *Poetry Speaks)* is meant to be a beginning, a starting point on a journey of discovery. For that reason, it is filled with range, historically, poetically, and visually. We hope you will use this book as a diving board, a place from which to plunge into the depths of poetry.

Some interesting facts about *Poetry Speaks to Children*:

- There are 95 poems in the book from 73 poets
- On the audio CD, you will find 50 poems from 34 poets, many of them recorded here for the first time

We are blessed to have most of the poems on the CD read by the poets themselves. You'll notice that sometimes the poets change the wording while they read—a testament to the fact that poetry lives and evolves. You will also find that for some readings, our poets provided a brief introduction—small stories, really—that we have included on the CD. You'll hear Langston Hughes explain how he wrote "The Negro Speaks of Rivers," one of his earliest poems, and Janet S. Wong tell you the story behind "Good Luck Gold." In some cases we've moved that introduction to its own track, prefacing the track of the poem itself.

Poetry Speaks to Children is an easy book to skip around in or dip into. The book and the audio are meant to be used together, but these kinds of rules are also meant to be broken. Use them together, separately, and in any way you wish! We have also included plenty of poems for you to read quietly or perform out loud or sing or chortle through. Enjoy!

Finally, we hope to hear from you. Please feel free to write and tell us what you thought of *Poetry Speaks to Children*. Tell us your favorite children's poem (from our book or another). And of course we'd love to know if our book took you further along the journey into poetry.

I welcome you now to *Poetry Speaks to Children*.

Dominique Raccah
Publisher

Introduction by Elise Paschen

On the cover of my favorite childhood book of poetry towers a magician, stirring a cauldron of poems, a raven perched on his arm. The cover is frayed and the pages are dog-eared. When I was young, I would pore over that book, rereading the poems, slipping into the illustrations. Inhabiting the world of the imagination, I would make myself at home in each of those poems.

Among my early favorites was William Blake's "The Tyger." I would utter the spell of the poem, over and over. My mother recalls, after I returned home from my third grade class one afternoon, how I proudly recited the poem, which begins: "Tyger! Tyger! burning bright/In the forests of the night,/What immortal hand or eye/Could frame thy fearful symmetry?" I remember puzzling over the word "symmetry," wondering what it meant and how it could rhyme with "eye." (Later it was explained that, during that time in England, the last syllable in "symmetry" was pronounced with a long "i" sound.) The incantatory elements of the poem mesmerized me: those pounding trochaic beats, the rhyming couplets, the repetition of the refrain. My curiosity was intrigued by the recurring questions, but, most of all, my imagination was ignited by the burning eyes of the tiger.

Many of us have our first encounter with language through poetry. As infants, we are held close to our parents' chests where we feel the beating of the heart, the undercurrent rhythm of poems. Many times, a child's first attempt at speech will incorporate rhyme—pronouncing first words that echo each other—"mama," "dada," "baba." As children grow older, they will chant their "ABCs," becoming familiar with the letters of the alphabet, later discovering how these letters assemble to form words. Letters become pieces of a puzzle as a child constructs and deconstructs the word. Oftentimes, children will learn to read by recognizing the family of sounds which reverberate; rhyme will help them understand how to piece words together.

I now can observe this universe of poetry for children from a new vantage point, as a mother of two young children. Every night, our daughter and son ask my husband and me to read "one more book, just one more book please." They love books, and we all treasure the end of the day when we snuggle together and read more stories under the covers. Before bedtime, my three-year-old son clutches a CD of songs which he, and our six-year-old daughter, will insert into the player, after which they prance around the living room, singing and dancing.

In *Poetry Speaks to Children* we decided to create something that would appeal to the eye and to the ear, featuring illustrated poems on the page accompanied by the voices of the poets on a CD. By introducing children to those visceral sounds and melodies of the spoken voice, we hope to spark their interest in poetry. We believe these poems will capture the imagination in the same way that songs captivate audiences young and old. We offer a vast array of voices—from Roald Dahl's "The Dentist and the Crocodile" to Gwendolyn Brooks' "The Tiger Who Wore White Gloves." But we also feature the voices of today's poets, from Joy Harjo to W. D. Snodgrass, who created original recordings for this book, recordings which we hope will lull, excite, and enchant in all their variety and musicality.

In the spirit of *Poetry Speaks* (a comprehensive selection of twentieth, and some nineteenth, century poetry for adults) we attempt to represent a diversity of voices and perspectives—from the anonymous Osage "I Rise, I Rise" to Richard Wilbur's opposite poems. We include short lyrics and long rambling narratives; old-time favorites, such as Edgar Allan Poe's "The Raven," as well as new poems written expressly for the book, like "Bear Song" by Kay Ryan. We try, most of all, to see the world, again, through children's eyes and present poems that tickle, give a scare; poems to mull over, ones that tell stories; some are earthbound, others, whimsical; finally several might even soothe to sleep. We want to offer all elements of a child's cosmos—from climbing trees to eating ice cream; from "How to Stay Up Late" to "How to Paint a Donkey"; from dogs and sheep to dinosaurs and unicorns; from mothers working to fathers tumbling into ponds.

We encourage children of all ages to dip into these pages, play the audio recordings, and discover your own favorites. We hope all these poems will captivate the imagination, but, even if just one takes root, then perhaps this book will have cast its own spell.

Elise Paschen

To ALL children (big and small) and the POETS within them,

ESPECIALLY
Alexandra, Stephen, Marie, Lyron, Doran, Gracie, Jimmers, Isabella and...

Madison, Sarah-Jessica, Griffin, Rhys, Jane, and Eden, Alex, Paul, Sherrie, Emily and Keaton, April, Joel, Morgan, Mary, Maxwell, Ashley, Geneva Michelle, Garrett, Gavin, Charlie, Zoe, Ignatius, Francis, Joseph, Nicholas (Nick), Xander, Spencer, Samuel, Simon, Mercedes, Audrey, Emily, Nicole, Paul, Luke, Anna, Mackenzie (Mack), Eden, Noah, Jack, Mike, Jeff, James, Jon, Charles (Chip), Caleb, Allison, Challen, Shawn, Megan, Erin, Carol, Connie, Susan, Nicholas, Alexander, Christopher, Katie, Alexandra, Nathan, Christopher John, Steven Edward, Matthew Frederick, Jacob Treebeard, Justice Major River, Amelia (Mia), Sarah, Wyatt, Audrey, Molly and Elie, Daniel Curtis, Dara, Matthew, Declan, Wesley, Wendy, Sheri, David, Scott, Tyler, Hannah, Dawn, Michelle, Billy, Kylie, Thomas and Matthew, Matt, Mark, David, Steven, Daniel, Paul, Katie, Sarah, Megan, Elissa, AnnaMarie, Glenna, Lauren, Reed, Michael, RaeMarie, Dana, Hannah, Grace, Jessie, Angie, Hannah, Rebekah, Sydney, JoAnna, Michael, John, Andrew, Cannon, Foster, Mia, Foster, Max, Ben, Ashley, Maya, Meghan and Madelyn, Alexandra, Keller, Elijah, Gimlet and Manfred, Gregory Paul, Annalee Beth, Caitlin Andrieanna, Rachel Mary Helen, Brandon Gregory, James Thornton, Theresa Lynn, Emma Mackenzie, Andrew, Sarah, Abigail, Cassandra, Caitlin Ione, Seth Michael, Braedon, Erik, Bart, Dannie, David, John, Janice, Eileen, Kristina, Ray, Patti, Molly, Morgan, Meredith, Lindsay, Lauren, Amanda, Nicholas, Preston, Quinten, Darby, Kayla, Jacob, Nathan, Elyse, Noah, Cecelia, Sylvie, Benjamin, Madelyn, Anna, Sophia, Kelly, Tracy, Victoria, Nathaniel, Douglas, Jennifer, Timothy, Isabel, Britt, John (Jack), Lindsey, Marianne, Caroline, Kenny, Stella, Isla, Jamie, Steven, Ella, Martin, James, Christopher, Christine, Theresa, Lisa, Joseph, Claire, Stewart, Jack, Josephine, Jerry, Patrice, Patricia, Robbie, Kelly, Bella, Georgina, Tomer, Alon, Amir, Ambreen, Leor, Ronen, Heinan, Melissa, Efraim, Yael, Meaghan, Kathryn, Lilian, Frances, George, Lucy, Jack, Carmella, Madeline, Robert, Spencer, Marsha, Paul, Jasper, Eleanor, Lauren, Noah, David Ethan, Leora Elizabeth, Harry Isiah, Mitchell, Benjamin, Jacob, Rudy, Samuel Benjamin, Robert Sterling, Lauren Claire, Sophia Elise, Bailey, Baxter, Mia, Grant, Kayla, Jacob, Brooke, Josh, Jeremy, China, Tia, Rio, Raven, Max, Nichole, Matthew, Emily, Alex, Corinne, Jeffery, Jessica, James, Timothy, Clara, Nathan, Daniel, Olivia, Paula, Schwartz, and Ian ...

and to the parents, librarians, and teachers who read with them.

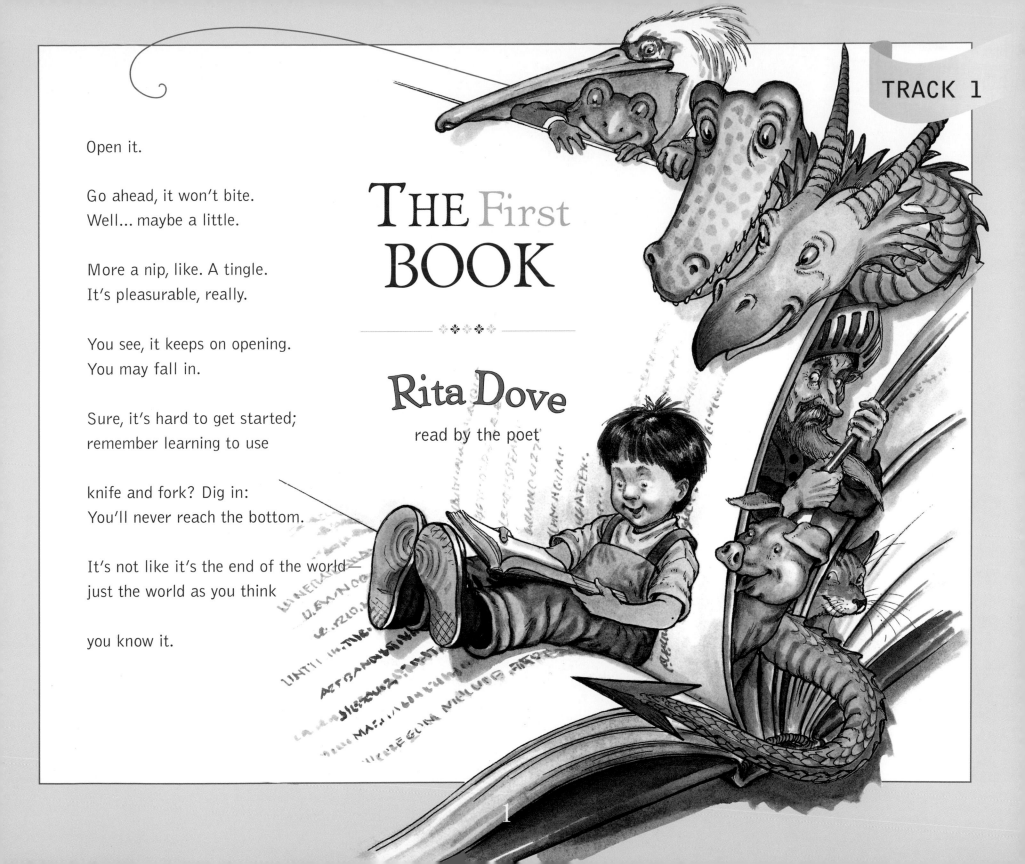

Open it.

Go ahead, it won't bite.
Well... maybe a little.

More a nip, like. A tingle.
It's pleasurable, really.

You see, it keeps on opening.
You may fall in.

Sure, it's hard to get started;
remember learning to use

knife and fork? Dig in:
You'll never reach the bottom.

It's not like it's the end of the world—
just the world as you think

you know it.

THE First BOOK

❖ ✳ ❖

Rita Dove

read by the poet

The QUARREL

✦ ✦ ✦

Maxine Kumin

read by the poet

Said a lightning bug to a firefly,
"Look at the lightning bugs fly by!"

"Silly dunce!" said the fly. "What bug ever flew?
Those are fireflies. And so are you."

"Bug!" cried the bug. "Fly!" cried the fly.
"Wait!" said a glowworm happening by.

"I'm a worm," squirmed the worm. "I glimmer all night.
You are worms, both of you. I know that I'm right."

"Fly!" cried the fly. "Worm!" cried the worm.
"Bug!" cried thc bug. "I'm standing firm!"

Back and forth through the dark each shouted his word
Till their quarrel awakened the early bird.

"You three noisy things, you are all related,"
She said to the worm, and promptly ate it.

With a snap of her bill she finished the fly,
And the lightning bug was the last to die.

All glowers and glimmerers, there's a MORAL:
Shine if you must, but do not quarrel.

Letter to Bee

Emily Dickinson

Bee! I'm expecting You!
Was saying Yesterday
To Somebody You know
That you were due—

The Frogs got Home last Week—
Are settled, and at work—
Birds, mostly back—
The Clover warm and thick—

You'll get my Letter by
The seventeenth; Reply
Or better, be with me—
Yours, Fly

Hurt no living thing;
Ladybird, nor butterfly,
Nor moth with dusty wing,
Nor cricket chirping cheerily,
Nor grasshopper so light of leap,
Nor dancing gnat, nor beetle fat,
Nor harmless worms that creep.

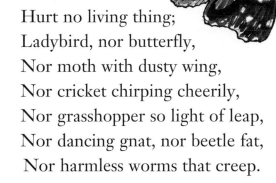

Hurt No Living Thing

Christina Rossetti

Stopping **by** WOODS **on** a Snowy Evening

Whose woods these are I think I know.
His house is in the village though;
He will not see me stopping here
To watch his woods fill up with snow.

My little horse must think it queer
To stop without a farmhouse near
Between the woods and frozen lake
The darkest evening of the year.

He gives his harness bells a shake
To ask if there is some mistake.
The only other sound's the sweep
Of easy wind and downy flake.

The woods are lovely, dark and deep,
But I have promises to keep,
And miles to go before I sleep,
And miles to go before I sleep.

Robert Frost
read by the poet

WOLF

❖ ❖

Billy Collins

read by the poet

A wolf is reading a book of fairy tales.
The moon hangs over the forest, a lamp.

He is not assuming a human position,
say, cross-legged against a tree,
as he would in a cartoon.

This is a real wolf, standing on all fours,
his rich fur bristling in the night air,
his head bent over the book open on the ground.

He does not sit down for the words
would be too far away to be legible,
and it is with difficulty that he turns
each page with his nose and forepaws.

When he finishes the last tale
he lies down in pine needles.
He thinks about what he has read,
the stories passing over his mind
like the clouds crossing the moon.

A zigzag of wind shakes down hazelnuts.
The eyes of owls yellow in the branches.

5

The **Tiger** WHO WORE White Gloves, OR, What You Are YOU ARE

✻ ✻ ✻

Gwendolyn Brooks

read by the poet

Brooks dedicated the poem to her children:
"For Nora Blakely, The First Tiger.
And for Henry Blakely, Jr; The Delineator."

There once was a tiger, terrible and tough,
who said "I don't think tigers are stylish enough.
They put on only orange and stripes of fierce black.
Fine and fancy fashion is what they mostly lack.
Even though they proudly
speak most loudly,
so that the jungle shakes
and every eye awakes—
Even though they slither
hither and thither
in such a wild way
that few may care to stay—
to be tough just isn't enough."
These things the tiger said,
And growled and tossed his head,
and rushed to the jungle fair
for something fine to wear.

Then!—what a hoot and yell
upon the jungle fell
The rhinoceros rasped!
The elephant gasped!
"By all that's sainted!"
said wolf—and fainted.

6

The crocodile cried.
The lion sighed.
The leopard sneered.
The jaguar jeered.
The antelope shouted.
The panther pouted.
Everyone screamed
"We never dreamed
that ever could be
in history
a tiger who loves
to wear white gloves.
White gloves are for girls
with manners and curls
and dresses and hats and bow-ribbons.
That's the way it always was
and rightly so, because
it's nature's nice decree
that tiger folk should be

not dainty, but daring,
and wisely wearing
what's fierce as the face,
not whiteness and lace!"

They shamed him and shamed him—
till none could have blamed him,
when at last, with a sigh
and a saddened eye,
and in spite of his love,
he took off each glove,
and agreed this was meant
all to prevail:
each tiger content
with his lashing tail
and satisfied
with his strong striped hide.

from

The
Adventures
OF
ISABEL

❊❊❊

Ogden Nash

read by the poet

One of Nash's daughters is named Isabel.

Isabel met an enormous bear,
Isabel, Isabel, didn't care;
The bear was hungry, the bear was ravenous,
The bear's big mouth was cruel and cavernous.
The bear said, "Isabel, glad to meet you,
How do, Isabel, now I'll eat you!"
Isabel, Isabel, didn't worry.
Isabel didn't scream or scurry.
She washed her hands and she straightened her hair up,
Then Isabel quietly ate the bear up.
Once in a night as black as pitch
Isabel met a wicked old witch.
The witch's face was cross and wrinkled,
The witch's gums with teeth were sprinkled.
"Ho, ho, Isabel!" the old witch crowed,
"I'll turn you into an ugly toad!"
Isabel, Isabel, didn't worry,

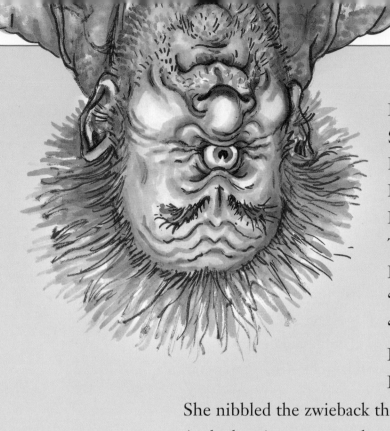

Isabel didn't scream or scurry,

She showed no rage and she showed no rancor,

But she turned the witch into milk and drank her.

Isabel met a hideous giant,

Isabel continued self-reliant.

The giant was hairy, the giant was horrid,

He had one eye in the middle of his forehead.

"Good morning, Isabel," the giant said,

"I'll grind your bones to make my bread."

Isabel, Isabel, didn't worry,

Isabel didn't scream or scurry.

She nibbled the zwieback that she always fed off,

And when it was gone, she cut the giant's head off.

Isabel met a troublesome doctor,

He punched and he poked till he really shocked her.

The doctor's talk was of coughs and chills

And the doctor's satchel bulged with pills.

The doctor said unto Isabel,

"Swallow this, it will make you well."

Isabel, Isabel, didn't worry,

Isabel didn't scream or scurry.

She took those pills from the pill concocter,

And Isabel calmly cured the doctor.

On A FLIMMERING Floom YOU Shall RIDE

Nobody noogers the shaff of a sloo.
Nobody slimbers a wench with a winch
Nor higgles armed each with a niggle
and each the flimdrat of a smee,
each the inbiddy hum of a smoo.

Then slong me dorst with the flagdarsh.
Then creep me deep with the crawbright.
Let idle winds ploodaddle the dorshes.
And you in the gold of the gloaming
You shall be sloam with the hoolriffs.

On a flimmering floom you shall ride.
They shall tell you bedish and desist.
On a flimmering floom you shall ride.

Carl Sandburg

El CHICLE

(for Marcel)

* * * * *

Ana Castillo

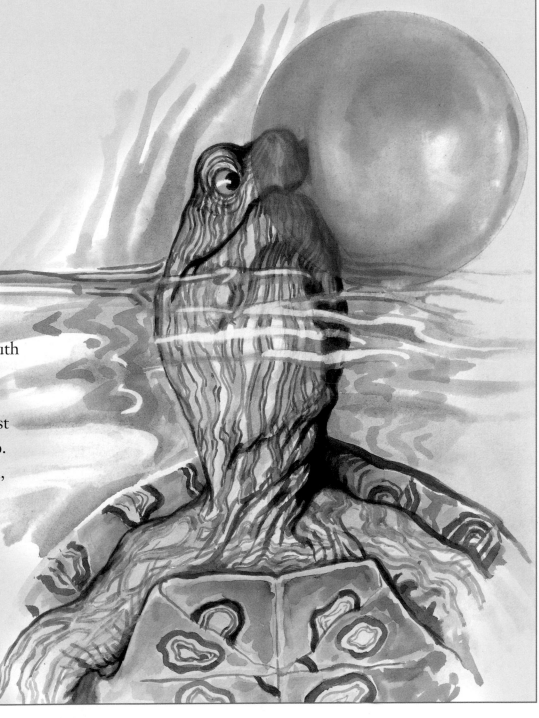

Mi'jo and I were laughing – *ha, ha, ha* –
when the gum he chewed fell out of his mouth
and into my hair which, after I clipped it,
flew in the air, on the back of a dragonfly
that dipped in the creek and was snapped fast
by a turtle that reached high and swam deep.
Mi'jo wondered what happened to that gum,
worried that it stuck to the back
of my seat and Mami will be mad when
she can't get it out. Meanwhile,
the turtle in the pond that ate the dragonfly
that carried the hair
with the gum on its back
swam South and hasn't been seen once
since.

THE Dentist and the Crocodile

Roald Dahl

read by the poet

The crocodile, with cunning smile, sat in the dentist's chair.
He said, "Right here and everywhere my teeth require repair."
The dentist's face was turning white. He quivered, quaked and shook.
He muttered, "I suppose I'm going to have to take a look."
"I want you," Crocodile declared, "to do the back ones first.
The molars at the very back are easily the worst."
He opened wide his massive jaws. It was a fearsome sight—
At least three hundred pointed teeth, all sharp and shining white.
The dentist kept himself well clear. He stood two yards away.
He chose the longest probe he had to search out the decay.
"I said to do the *back ones* first!" the Crocodile called out.
"You're much too far away, dear sir, to see what you're about.
To do the back ones properly you've got to put your head
Deep down inside my great big mouth," the grinning Crocky said.
The poor old dentist wrung his hands and, weeping in despair,
He cried, "No no! I see them all extremely well from here!"
Just then, in burst a lady, in her hands a golden chain.
She cried, "Oh Croc, you naughty boy, you're playing tricks again!"
"Watch out!" the dentist shrieked and started climbing up the wall.
"He's after me! He's after you! He's going to eat us all!"
"Don't be a twit," the lady said, and flashed a gorgeous smile.
"He's harmless. He's my little pet, my lovely crocodile."

If I were a bear
with a bear sort of belly

that made it hard
to get up after sitting

and if I had paws
with pads on the ends

and a kind of a tab
where a tail might begin

and a button eye
on each side of my nose

I'd button the flap
of the forest closed.

And when you came
with your wolf and your stick

to the place that once was
the place to get in

you'd simply be
at the edge of the town

and your wolf wouldn't know
a bear was around.

Bear Song

❖❖❖❖❖

Kay Ryan

read by the poet

13

Jabberwocky

✦✦✦

Lewis Carroll

read by Emma Fielding

Lewis Carroll wrote the famous nonsense poem "Jabberwocky" for his story about Alice, *Through The Looking Glass*. Carroll used a lot of new made-up words in the poem, and yet you still understand the story. Alice says to Humpty Dumpty about "Jabberwocky," "Somehow it seems to fill my head with ideas—only I don't exactly know what they are!"

'Twas brillig, and the slithy toves
    Did gyre and gimble in the wabe:
All mimsy were the borogoves,
    And the mome raths outgrabe.

"Beware the Jabberwock, my son!
    The jaws that bite, the claws that catch!
Beware the Jubjub bird, and shun
    The frumious Bandersnatch!"

He took his vorpal sword in hand:
    Long time the manxome foe he sought—
So rested he by the Tumtum tree,
    And stood awhile in thought.

And, as in uffish thought he stood,
    The Jabberwock, with eyes of flame,
Came whiffing through the tulgey wood,
    And burbled as it came!

One, two! One, two! And through and through
    The vorpal blade went snicker-snack!
He left it dead, and with its head
    He went galumphing back.

"And hast thou slain the Jabberwock?
    Come to my arms, my beamish boy!
O frabjous day! Callooh! Callay!"
    He chortled in his joy.

'Twas brillig, and the slithy toves
    Did gyre and gimble in the wabe:
All mimsy were the borogoves,
    And the mome raths outgrabe.

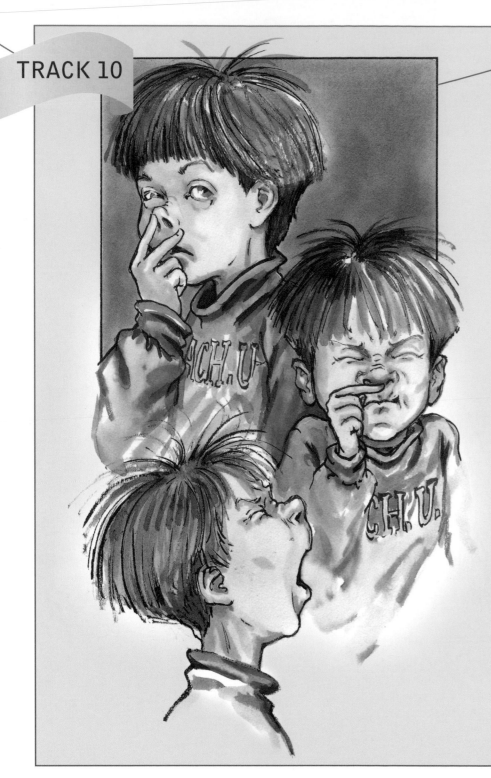

There's a
sort of a
tickle
the size of a
nickel,
a bit like the
prickle
of sweet-sour
pickle,

it's a
quivery
shiver
the shape of a
sliver,
like eels in a
river,

a kind of a
wiggle
that starts as a
jiggle
and joggles
its way to a
tease,

which I
cannot
suppress
any longer,
I guess,
so pardon me,
please,
while I
sneeze.

SNEEZE

Maxine Kumin

read by the poet

Mrs. Mitchell's underwear
    Is dancing on the line;
Mrs. Mitchell's underwear
    Has never looked so fine.

Mrs. Mitchell hates to dance—
    She says it's not refined,
But Mrs. Mitchell's underwear
    Is prancing on the line.

With a polka-dotted polka
    And a tangled tango too,
Mrs. Mitchell's underwear
    Is like a frilly zoo!

Mrs. Mitchell's
UNDERWEAR

Dennis Lee

Okay,
Brown GIRL,
OKAY

For Josie (9 years old, who wrote to me saying...
"boys called me names because of my color.
I felt very upset... My brother and sister are English.
I wish I was, then I won't be picked on... How do
you like being brown?")

❖❖❖❖❖

James Berry

read by the poet

18

Josie, Josie, I am okay
being brown. I remember,
every day dusk and dawn get born
from the loving of night and light
who work together, like married.
   And they would like to say to you:
   Be at school on and on, brown Josie
   like thousands and thousands and thousands
   of children, who are brown and white
   and black and pale-lemon color.
   All the time, brown girl Josie is okay.

Josie, Josie, I am okay
being brown. I remember,
every minute sun in the sky
and ground of the earth work together
like married.
   And they would like to say to you:
   Ride on up a going escalator
   like thousands and thousands and thousands
   of people, who are brown and white
   and black and pale-lemon color.
   All the time, brown girl Josie is okay.

Josie, Josie, I am okay
being brown. I remember,
all the time bright-sky and brown-earth
work together, like married
making forests and food and flowers and rain.
   And they would like to say to you:
   Grow and grow brightly, brown girl.
   Write and read and play and work.
   Ride bus or train or boat or airplane
   like thousands and thousands and thousands
   of people, who are brown and white
   and black and pale-lemon color.
   All the time, brown girl Josie is okay.

TRACK 13

Vowel OWL

(Roger)

John Hollander

read by the poet

"OO-ih, oo-oooo!"
"Oo-ih, oo-oooo!"
Something is missing from the sound
Outside the window, in the frost.
"Oo-ih, oo-oooo!"
"Oo-ih, oo-oooo!"
All the "oo's" are very round
But somehow all the "t's" got lost.
Poor Roger knows how poets wrote
That owls are always singing out
"Too-whit, Too-whoo, a merry note"
He does his best, beyond a doubt.
(Roger is really good as gold.)
But unlike other owls,
He only howls in vowels.

Perhaps he has a cold.

MAGIC
WORDS

after Nalungiaq

In the very earliest time,
when both people and animals lived on earth,
a person could become an animal if he wanted to
and an animal could become a human being.
Sometimes they were people
and sometimes animals
and there was no difference.
All spoke the same language.
That was the time when words were like magic.
The human mind had mysterious powers.
A word spoken by chance
might have strange consequences.
It would suddenly come alive
and what people wanted to happen could happen—
all you had to do was say it.
Nobody could explain this:
That's the way it was.

translated by Edward Field

The Unwritten

Inside this pencil
crouch words that have never been written
never been spoken
never been taught

they're hiding

what script can it be
that they won't unroll
in what language
would I recognize it
would I be able to follow it
to make out the real names
of everything

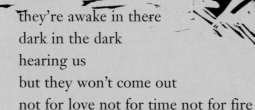

they're awake in there
dark in the dark
hearing us
but they won't come out
not for love not for time not for fire

maybe there aren't
many

even when the dark has worn away
they'll still be there
hiding in the air
multitudes in days to come may walk through them
breathe them
be none the wiser

it could be that there's only one word
and it's all we need
it's here in this pencil

every pencil in the world
is like this

W.S. Merwin

This box contains the wash of blue sky,
spikes of green spring,
a circle of yellow sun,
triangle flames of orange and red.

It has the lime caterpillar
inching on a brown branch,
the shadow black in the center
of a grove of trees.

It holds my pink
and your chocolate
and her burnt sienna
and his ivory skin.

In it are all the colors of the world.

All the colors of the world.

Crayons:
A RAINBOW
Poem

❖❖❖❖

Jane Yolen

GAS

❖❖❖❖❖

C. K. Williams

The poet wrote "Gas" for his grandchildren.

There's a land called France
that has an odd law,
a law that might make you
drop your jaw,
for what it proclaims
in words very clear,
is that FARTING
IS FORBIDDEN HERE.

Did you say FARTING?
Did you say FORBIDDEN?

Yes, it's true,
there's a country called France
in which farting
must be HIDDEN,
　BECAUSE FARTING
　　IN FRANCE
　　IS FORBIDDEN!

TOOT!

Though it's not so in Canada,
and not in Spain,
and not on the prairie,
and not on the plain,
and not in countries like Egypt
where camels are ridden,
in France,
on the rivers and mountains,
on the roads and in fields,
FARTING IS FORBIDDEN!

Will a policeman arrest you
in France
if you fart?
Nobody knows,
but he might blow his whistle,
or pinch your toes.

So what should you say
if a policeman in France
asks, DID YOU FART?
You should answer
as quickly as you can,
"THAT WASN'T ME,
IT WAS MY BROTHER!"

And what should your brother
say if *he's* asked
DID YOU FART?
Why, he should reply,
"THAT WAS MY OTHER,
LITTLER BROTHER!"

And what about him
your baby brother,
what should he say
if someone asks him,
DID YOU FART?

Well, he won't answer,
because he can't talk,
though it's well known
that babies fart
before they can walk!

We pretend that we don't,
and cover our nose,
but it's really a pose
because everyone knows
that EVERYONE FARTS:
Fathers and mothers,
and sisters and brothers,
grandmas and grandpas,
and babies who goo.

So if one day in France
a policeman
or not even a policeman
should inquire of you,
"Excuse me, DID YOU FART?
DID YOUR BROTHERS FART, TOO?"

Without hesitation,
you and your brothers
must shout:
"IT'S NOT US WHO FARTED,
YOU SILLY PERSON,
IT WAS *YOU*!"

KNITTED
Things

Karla Kuskin

There was a witch who knitted things:
Elephants and playground swings.
She knitted rain,
She knitted night,
But nothing really came out right.
The elephants had just one tusk
And night looked more
Like dawn or dusk.
The rain was snow
And when she tried
To knit an egg
It came out fried.
She knitted birds
With buttonholes
And twenty rubber butter rolls.
She knitted blue angora trees.
She purl stitched countless purple fleas.
She knitted a palace in need of a darn.
She knitted a battle and ran out of yarn.
She drew out a strand
Of her gleaming, green hair
And knitted a lawn
Till she just wasn't there.

Double, double toil and trouble;
Fire burn, and cauldron bubble.
Fillet of a fenny snake,
In the cauldron boil and bake;
Eye of newt and toe of frog,
Wool of bat and tongue of dog,
Adder's fork and blind-worm's sting,
Lizard's leg and howlet's wing,
For a charm of powerful trouble,
Like a hell-broth boil and bubble.
Double, double toil and trouble;
Fire burn, and cauldron bubble.

from
MACBEATH

William Shakespeare

Some playwrights include poems in their plays. William Shakespeare's three witches recite a spell over a cauldron in a dark cave in *Macbeth*, Act 4, Scene 1, and the spell works as a poem.

Frodo's SONG in Bree

❉ ❉

J. R. R. Tolkien

There is an inn, a merry old inn
beneath an old grey hill,
And there they brew a beer so brown
That the Man in the Moon himself came down
one night to drink his fill.

The ostler has a tipsy cat
that plays a five-stringed fiddle;
And up and down he runs his bow,
Now squeaking high, now purring low,
now sawing in the middle.

The landlord keeps a little dog
that is mighty fond of jokes;
When there's good cheer among the guests,
He cocks an ear at all the jests
and laughs until he chokes.

They also keep a hornéd cow
as proud as any queen;
But music turns her head like ale,
And makes her wave her tufted tail
and dance upon the green.

This poem appears in
The Fellowship of the Ring, the first
book in Tolkien's *Lord of the Rings* trilogy.

And O! the rows of silver dishes
and the store of silver spoons!
For Sunday there's a special pair,
And these they polish up with care
on Saturday afternoons.

The Man in the Moon was drinking deep,
and the cat began to wail;
A dish and a spoon on the table danced,
The cow in the garden madly pranced,
and the little dog chased his tail.

The Man in the Moon took another mug,
and then rolled beneath his chair;
And there he dozed and dreamed of ale,
Till in the sky the stars were pale,
and dawn was in the air.

Then the ostler said to his tipsy cat:
"The white horses of the Moon,
They neigh and champ their silver bits;
But their master's been and drowned his wits,
and the Sun'll be rising soon!"

So the cat on the fiddle played hey-diddle-diddle,
a jig that would wake the dead;
He squeaked and sawed and quickened the tune,
While the landlord shook the Man in the Moon:
"It's after three!" he said.

They rolled the Man slowly up the hill
and bundled him into the Moon,
While his horses galloped up in rear,
And the cow came capering like a deer,
and a dish ran up with the spoon.

Now quicker the fiddle went deedle-dum-diddle;
the dog began to roar,
The cow and the horses stood on their heads;
The guests all bounded from their beds
and danced upon the floor.

With a ping and a pang the fiddle-strings broke!
the cow jumped over the Moon,
And the little dog laughed to see such fun,
And the Saturday dish went off at a run
with the silver Sunday spoon.

The round Moon rolled behind the hill,
as the Sun raised up her head.
She hardly believed her fiery eyes;
For though it was day, to her surprise
they all went back to bed!

EAGLE Poem

❖❖❖

Joy Harjo

read by the poet

Harjo writes, "In classical native traditions, songs are the most common source of poetry. Wherever words appear, they are not very far away from song or dance."

To pray you open your whole self
To sky, to earth, to sun, to moon
To one whole voice that is you.
And know there is more
That you can't see, can't hear,
Can't know except in moments
Steadily growing, and in languages
That aren't always sound but other
Circles of motion.
Like eagle that Sunday morning
Over Salt River. Circled in blue sky
In wind, swept our hearts clean
With sacred wings.
We see you, see ourselves and know
That we must take the utmost care
And kindness in all things.
Breathe in, knowing we are made of
All this, and breathe, knowing
We are truly blessed because we
Were born, and die soon within a
True circle of motion,
Like eagle rounding out the morning
Inside us.
We pray that it will be done
In beauty.
In beauty.

The Negro SPEAKS of RIVERS

(To W.E.B. DuBois)

I've known rivers:
I've known rivers ancient as the world and older than
    the flow of human blood in human veins.

My soul has grown deep like the rivers.

I bathed in the Euphrates when dawns were young.
I built my hut near the Congo and it lulled me to sleep.
I looked upon the Nile and raised the pyramids above
    it.
I heard the singing of the Mississippi when Abe Lincoln
    went down to New Orleans, and I've seen its muddy
    bosom turn all golden in the sunset.

I've known rivers:
Ancient, dusky rivers.

My soul has grown deep like the rivers.

❖❖❖❖

Langston Hughes

read by the poet

This is an early Hughes poem, written when he was eighteen years old
and traveling on a train to Mexico to visit his father.

31

I Rise, I Rise

From an Osage prayer before
a young man's first buffalo hunt.

Anonymous Osage Poet

I rise, I rise,
I, whose tread makes the earth to rumble.
I rise, I rise,
I, in whose thighs there is strength.
I rise, I rise,
I, who whips his back with his tail when in rage.
I rise, I rise,
I, in whose humped shoulder there is power.
I rise, I rise,
I, who shakes his mane when angered.
I rise, I rise,
I, whose horns are sharp and curved.

I keep six honest serving-men
    (They taught me all I knew);
Their names are What and Why and When
    And How and Where and Who.
I send them over land and sea,
    I send them east and west;
But after all they have worked for me,
    I give them all a rest.

I let them rest from nine till five,
    For I am busy then,
As well as breakfast, lunch and tea,
    For they are hungry men.
But different folk have different views.
    I know a person small—
She keeps ten million serving-men,
    Who get no rest at all!

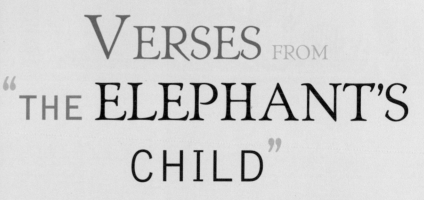

She sends 'em abroad on her own affairs,
    From the second she opens her eyes—
One million Hows, two million Wheres,
    And seven million Whys!

Verses from "The Elephant's Child"

Rudyard Kipling

The poet wrote this for his daughter,
Elsie, who was always asking "why?"

ALPHABETS.
part 1

✳ ✳

Seamus Heaney

A shadow his father makes with joined hands
And thumbs and fingers nibbles on the wall
Like a rabbit's head. He understands
He will understand more when he goes to school.

There he draws smoke with chalk the whole first week,
Then draws the forked stick that they call a Y.
This is writing. A swan's neck and swan's back
Make the 2 he can see now as well as say.

Two rafters and a cross-tie on the slate
Are the letter some call *ah*, some call *ay*.
There are charts, there are headlines, there is a right
Way to hold the pen and a wrong way.

First it is "copying out," and then "English"
Marked correct with a little leaning hoe.
Smells of inkwells rise in the classroom hush.
A globe in the window tilts like a colored O.

John Smith and his son, John Smith,
     And his son's son John, and-a-one
     And-a-two and-a-three
And-a-rum-tum-tum, and-a
Lean John, and his son, lean John,
     And his lean son's John, and-a-one
     And-a-two and-a-three
And-a-drum-rum-rum, and-a
Rich John, and his son, rich John,
     And his rich son's John, and-a-one
     And-a-two and-a-three
And-a-pom-pom-pom, and-a-
Wise John, and his son, wise John,
     And his wise son's John, and-a-one
     And-a-two and-a-three
And-a-fee and-a-fee and-a-fee
     And-a-fee-fo-fum—
Voilà la vie, la vie, la vie,
     And-a-rummy-tummy-tum
     And-a-rummy-tummy-tum.

John SMITH
and his son
JOHN Smith

✳✳✳

Wallace Stevens

About the TEETH of SHARKS

※ ※ ※

John Ciardi

read by the poet

The thing about a shark is—teeth,
One row above, one row beneath.

Now take a close look. Do you find
It has another row behind?

Still closer—here, I'll hold your hat:
Has it a third row behind that?

Now look in and... Look out! Oh my,
I'll *never* know now! Well, goodbye.

Dinosaur DIETS

* * * * *

Jane Yolen

Stegosaurus fed on ferns,
The sauropods on pine,
Tyrannosaurus ate them both,
Whenever he did dine.

So he was not invited
Very often out to lunch
Because he chose upon his hosts
To munch

and crunch

a bunch.

My sister saw a dinosaur.
At least she said she saw one.
I said that dinosaurs are dead.
She said she saw it in her head.
A dinosaur inside your head?
"Remarkable!" my mother said.

My Sister SAW A Dinosaur

* * * * *

Mary Ann Hoberman

read by the poet

37

Listen to the poet describe how to make an alphabet book.
It might be fun to write your own!

JOEY

❖ ❖

Brad Leithauser

read by the poet

A baby kangaroo is called a joey.
His early life's a little vertigo-y
Since Mama's always bouncing like a ball.
She doesn't stop to wonder what effect
The bouncing's having on his brain; in fact,
      She doesn't stop at all.
           kid'll   cope?)
(Surely the   learn to
She's like a kid herself—forever jumping rope.

A rabbit
bit
A little bit
An itty-bitty
Little bit of beet.
Then bit
By bit
He bit
Because he liked the taste of it.
But when he bit
A wee bit more,
It was more bitter than before.
"This beet is bitter!"
Rabbit cried.
"I feel a bit unwell inside!"
But when he bit
Another bite, that bit of beet
Seemed quite all right.
Besides
When all is said and done,
Better bitter beet
Than none.

How many *bits* can you find?

Rabbit

Mary Ann Hoberman

read by the poet

39

At Last

✦ ✦

James Stevenson

Dogs go in the back seat,
Always in the back seat,
Miles in the back seat,
Hours in the back seat.

But in the parking lots of shopping centers,
You'll see: Dogs get their chance
At last
To drive.

Epigram Engraved on the Collar of a Dog Which I Gave to His Royal Highness

I am his Highness' dog at Kew;
Pray tell me, sir, whose dog are you?

✦ ✦

Alexander Pope

40

BALLOONS

Balloons in the attic, balloons on the roof,
Punch 'em with a pin, they go Poof! Poof! Poof!
Balloons in the driveway, balloons on the lawn.
Poof! Poof! Poof!   Balloons all gone!

Horses on the racetrack, horses in the stable,
Chickens in the cherry trees, chickens on the table,
Bats in the belfry, bats in the barn.
Bats! Bats! Bats!

                    Howling cats!

                              Ladies, hold your hats!

          Poof! Poof! Poof!

                    Galloping Goof!

Look at that elephant up on the roof—

          He's about to jump…

HE JUMPED!

          READ ON!

William Jay Smith

read by the poet

41

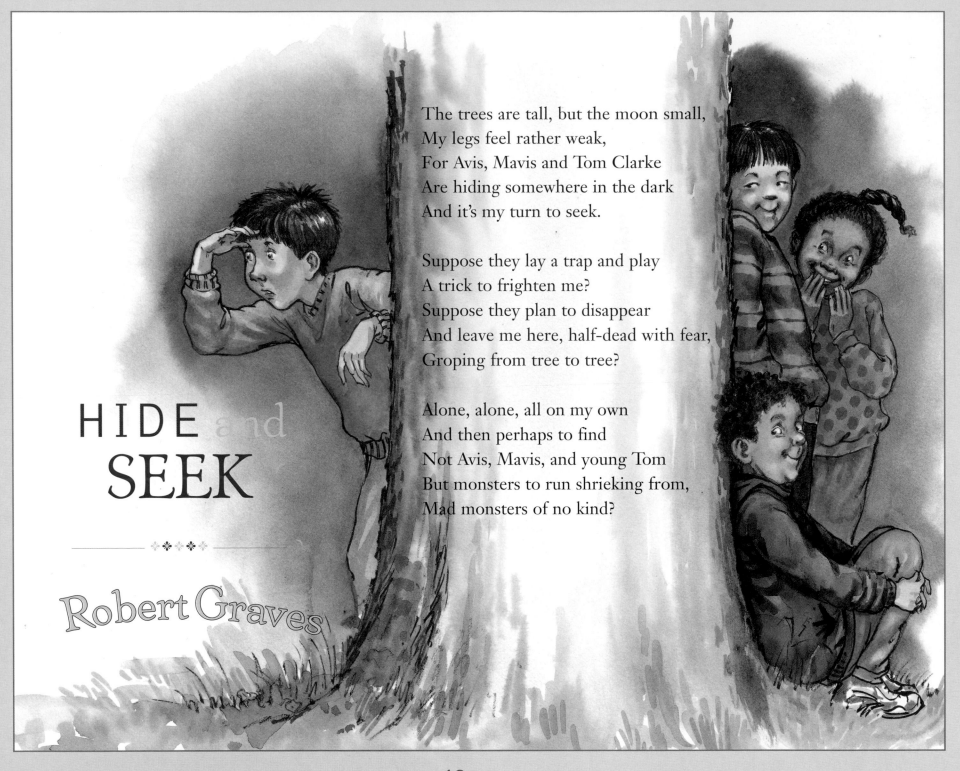

HIDE and SEEK

Robert Graves

The trees are tall, but the moon small,
My legs feel rather weak,
For Avis, Mavis and Tom Clarke
Are hiding somewhere in the dark
And it's my turn to seek.

Suppose they lay a trap and play
A trick to frighten me?
Suppose they plan to disappear
And leave me here, half-dead with fear,
Groping from tree to tree?

Alone, alone, all on my own
And then perhaps to find
Not Avis, Mavis, and young Tom
But monsters to run shrieking from,
Mad monsters of no kind?

Every time I climb a tree
Every time I climb a tree
Every time I climb a tree
I scrape a leg
Or skin a knee
And every time I climb a tree
I find some ants
Or dodge a bee
And get the ants
All over me

And every time I climb a tree
Where have you been?
They say to me
But don't they know that I am free
Every time I climb a tree?
I like it best
To spot a nest
That has an egg
Or maybe three

And then I skin
The other leg
But every time I climb a tree
I see a lot of things to see
Swallows rooftops and TV
And all the fields and farms there be
Every time I climb a tree
Though climbing may be good for ants
It isn't especially good for pants
But still it's pretty good for me
Every time I climb a tree

Every Time
I Climb a Tree

* * * *

David McCord

Nikki Giovanni

read by the poet

The Reason
I Like Chocolate

The reason I like chocolate
is I can lick my fingers
and nobody tells me I'm not polite

I especially like scary movies
'cause I can snuggle with my mommy
or my big sister and they don't laugh

I like to cry sometimes 'cause
everybody says, "What's the matter
don't cry"

and I like books
for all those reasons
but mostly 'cause they just make me
happy

and I really like
to be happy

44

Trips

eeeveryyee time

when i take my bath

and comb my hair (i mean

mommy brushes it till i almost cry)

and put on my clean clothes

and they all say MY

HOW NICE YOU LOOK

and i smile and say

"thank you mommy cleaned

me up"

then i sit down and mommy says

GET UP FROM THERE YOU GONNA BE DIRTY

'FORE I HAVE A CHANCE TO GET DRESSED
  MYSELF

and i want to tell her if you was

my size the dirt would catch

you up faster too

"Poems are, to me, little stories, snapshots of a moment, little gumdrops,
pieces of light, laughter in a crystal. I love these poems because
they, all of them, capture the wonder and courage; the little girl was
exasperated (though she would not know that word) that she got dirty
again so quickly and mother was so upset. I like those moments in a
bottle—a breeze, a giggle."

—Nikki Giovanni

MOMMIES

MOMMIES

make you brush your teeth

and put your old clothes on

and clean the room

and call you from the playground

and fuss at daddies and uncles

and tuck you in at night

and kiss you

45

LINEAGE

✦✦✦✦✦

Margaret Walker

My grandmothers were strong.
They followed plows and bent to toil.
They moved through fields sowing seed.
They touched earth and grain grew.
They were full of sturdiness and singing.
My grandmothers were strong.

My grandmothers are full of memories
Smelling of soap and onions and wet clay
With veins rolling roughly over quick hands
They have many clean words to say.
My grandmothers were strong.
Why am I not as they?

My ancestor, a man
of Himalayan snow,
came to Kashmir from Samarkand,
carrying a bag
of whale bones.
His skeleton
carved from glaciers, his breath
arctic,
he froze women in his embrace.
His wife thawed into stony water,
her old age a clear
evaporation.

This heirloom,
his skeleton under my skin, passed
from son to grandson,
generations of snowmen on my back.
They tap every year on my window,
their voices hushed to ice.

No, they won't let me out of winter,
and I've promised myself,
even if I'm the last snowman,
That I'll ride into spring
on their melting shoulders.

SNOWMEN

Agha Shahid Ali

When I was a baby,
one month old,
my grandparents gave me
good luck gold:
a golden ring
so soft it bends,
a golden necklace
hooked at the ends,
a golden bracelet
with coins that say
I will be rich
and happy someday.
I wish that gold
would work
real soon.
I need my luck
this afternoon.

GOOD LUCK Gold

* * *

Janet S. Wong

read by the poet

Janet Wong's grandparents gave her good luck gold when she was one month old at a red egg and ginger party. She still has it and feels lucky.

48

Who saw the petals
    drop from the rose?
I, said the spider,
But nobody knows.

Who saw the sunset
    flash on a bird?
I, said the fish,
But nobody heard.

Who saw the fog
    come over the sea?
I, said the sea pigeon,
Only me.

Who saw the first
    green light of the sun?
I, said the night owl,
The only one.

Who saw the moss
    creep over the stone?
I, said the gray fox,
All alone.

The Secret SONG

Margaret Wise Brown

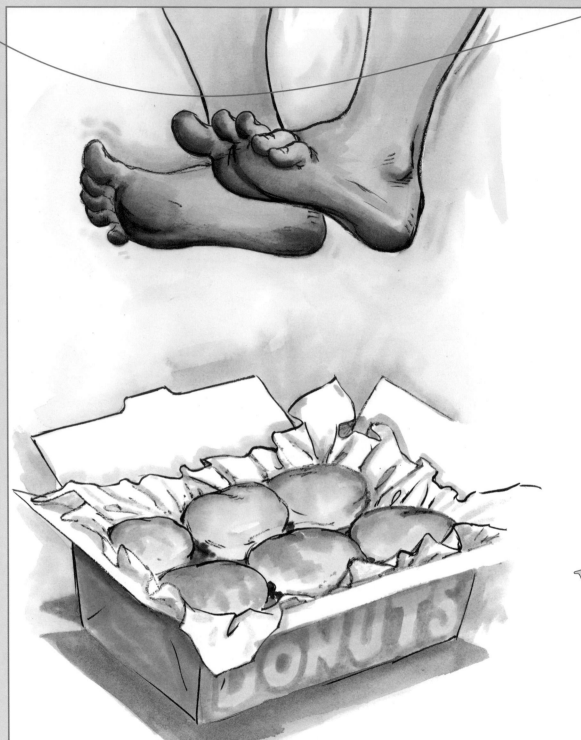

Why is it…
While other people
Are thinking about all kinds of
Important things…
I am thinking about
What it would be like
To jump barefoot
Into an open box
Of jelly doughnuts?

WHY?

❖❖❖❖

James Stevenson

The
Question

Karla Kuskin

People always say to me
"What do you think you'd like to be
When you grow up?"
And I say "Why,
I think I'd like to be the sky
Or be a plane or train or mouse
Or maybe a haunted house
Or something furry, rough and wild...
Or maybe I will stay a child."

In the play Amy didn't want to be
Anybody; so she managed the curtain.
Sharon wanted to be Amy. But Sam
wouldn't let anybody be anybody else—
he said it was wrong. "All right," Steve said,
"I'll be me but I don't like it."
So Amy was Amy, and we didn't have the play.
And Sharon cried.

FIRST GRADE

❋ ❋ ❋ ❋

William Stafford

Crying only a little bit
is no use. You must cry
until your pillow is soaked!
Then you can get up and laugh.
Then you can jump in the shower
and splash-splash-splash!
Then you can throw open your window
and, "Ha ha! Ha ha!"
And if people say, "Hey,
what's going on up there?"
"Ha ha!" sing back, "Happiness
was hiding in the last tear!
I wept it! Ha ha!"

Crying

✦✦✦✦✦

Galway Kinnell

read by the poet

Ms. Beecher said I don't know how
　　To make a lifelike tree.
Well, all I did was look and draw
　　How branches looked to me.

I *know* what you're supposed to do—
　　You make a Y, and sitting
On both its arms another two
　　Y's. Make them go on splitting.

I went and looked up at a bough
　　With bark like scraped black leather,
And neither does a tree know how
　　To fit a tree together.

ART CLASS

✦✦✦

X. J. Kennedy

read by the poet

54

HOW to Paint a Donkey

✻✻✻

Naomi Shihab Nye

read by the poet

She said the head was too large,
the hooves too small.

I could clean my paintbrush
but I couldn't get rid of that voice.

While they watched,
I crumpled him,

let his blue body
stain my hand.

I cried when he hit the can.
She smiled. I could try again.

Maybe this is what I unfold in the dark,
deciding, for the rest of my life,

that donkey was just the right size.

DADDY Fell INTO the Pond

*****

Alfred Noyes

Everyone grumbled. The sky was grey.
We had nothing to do and nothing to say.
We were nearing the end of a dismal day,
And there seemed to be nothing beyond,
                    THEN
Daddy fell into the pond!

And everyone's face grew merry and bright,
And Timothy danced for sheer delight.
"Give me the camera, quick, oh quick!
He's crawling out of the duckweed." *Click!*

Then the gardener suddenly slapped his knee,
And doubled up, shaking silently,
And the ducks all quacked as if they were daft
And it sounded as if the old drake laughed.

O, there wasn't a thing that didn't respond
                    WHEN
Daddy fell into the pond!

Some of the time
I get on the bus
with mother

(just the two of us)

and we go to the place
where she works all day.

We take some games
so I can play,

and some of the time
I help a lot
with work that mother

just forgot —
(or couldn't finish —
or did all wrong —)

It's good
she needs me
to come along.

Working with
MOTHER

——— ✦✦✦✦ ———

Myra Cohn Livingston

A FAERY Song

Sung by the people of Faery over Diarmuid and Grania,
in their bridal sleep under a Cromlech.

We who are old, old and gay,
O so old!
Thousands of years, thousands of years,
If all were told:

Give to these children, new from the world,
Silence and love;
And the long dew-dropping hours of the night,
And the stars above:

Give to these children, new from the world,
Rest far from men.
Is anything better, anything better?
Tell us it then:

Us who are old, old and gay,
O so old!
Thousands of years, thousands of years,
If all were told.

❖❖❖❖

read by Paul Muldoon

translated by Paul Muldoon

The UNICORN

❖❖❖❖❖

Rainer Maria Rilke

read by Paul Muldoon

This, then, is the beast that has never actually been:
not having seen one, they prized in any case
its perfect poise, its throat, the straightforward gaze
it gave them back—so straightforward, so serene.

Since it had never been, it was all the more
unsullied. And they allowed it such latitude
that, in a clearing in the wood,
it raised its head as if its essence shrugged off mere

existence. They brought it on, not with oats or corn,
but with the chance, however slight,
that it might come on its own. This gave it such strength

that from its brow there sprang a horn. A single horn.
Only when it met a maiden's white with white
would it be bodied out in her, in her mirror's full length.

The Lion and THE LILY

Elizabeth Spires

read by the poet

A lion met a lily
out walking one day.
The wind was blowing gently,
and the lily bowed and swayed.

Roared the lion to the lily,
"Why do you bend that way?
Don't let a little breeze
push you around!"

"It's my nature to bow,"
the sweet lily sighed.
"I couldn't stand my ground
even if I tried."

"Hmmmm," said the lion,
a dark thought coming over him.
"I could tear you with my teeth.
Beg me not to."

"About Fate, I take
the large view," the lily replied.
"Why should I plead for my life
when you'll do what you'll do?"

"That's true," agreed the lion.
"I have you in my power."
But secretly he marveled
at the cunning of the flower.

The lily went on. "I envy you, really,
that ruff of fur, those claws,
and how the forest trembles
when you roar your terrible roars."

O the lily was wily,
No doubt about that.
To speak so poetically
to an unpoetic cat.

"Sometimes I'd like to be . . .
you," the lily confessed.
"Four feet on the ground
and always so self-possessed."

"On the other hand," said the lion,
"it must be gratifying
to have everyone love you,
to be the beautiful one."

"Well, yes, it can be,"
the lily admitted.
"But also a little limiting.
"I want to be more than beautiful —

"— and I want to be more
than king!" the lion chimed in.
Now something was happening
that neither could explain.

The lion's claws retracted.
His cheeks were hot and flushed.
The lily's snow-white pallor
took on a pinkish blush.

"Is this what Keats felt?"
the lion asked himself.
Then stopped amazed
at his own poetic thought.

"We'd make a strange sight,"
said the lily quietly.
"A lily with a lion . . .
what would the flowers say?"

The lily stood there nakedly,
Without shield or sword.
And the lion bowed down,
And they both adored.

And the lily felt powerful,
And the lion gentle and small,
As they walked off together
in each other's thrall.

61

HIST WHIST

✦ ✦ ✦

e. e. cummings

hist   whist
little ghostthings
tip-toe
twinkle-tope

little twitchy
witches and tingling
goblins
hob-a-nob   hob-a-nob

little hoppy happy
toad in tweeds
tweeds
little itchy mousies

with scuttling
eyes   rustle and run   and
hidehidehide
whisk

whisk   look out for the old woman
with the wart on her nose
what she'll do to yer
nobody knows

for she knows the devil   ooch
the devil   ouch
the devil
ach   the great

green
dancing
devil
devil

devil
devil

wheeEEE

62

The Ghost
AND Jenny Jemima

❖❖❖

Dennis Lee

performed by Eddie Douglas

On the CD, listen to how the
poem's title becomes the song's chorus.

The clock struck one,
The clock struck two,
The ghost came playing
Peekaboo.

The clock struck three,
The clock struck four,
and Jenny Jemima
Began to roar.

The clock struck five,
The clock struck six,
The ghost could walk through
Steel and bricks.

The clock struck seven,
The clock struck eight,
And Jenny Jemima's
Hair stood straight.

The clock struck nine,
The clock struck ten…

The ghost wound the clock
and went home again.

FROM
The RAVEN

Edgar Allan Poe

This poem is read by Basil Rathbone,
perhaps best known for his portrayal of Sherlock Holmes.

Once upon a midnight dreary, while I pondered, weak and weary,
Over many a quaint and curious volume of forgotten lore—
While I nodded, nearly napping, suddenly there came a tapping,
As of someone gently rapping, rapping at my chamber door.
" 'Tis some visitor," I muttered, "tapping at my chamber door—
> Only this and nothing more."

Ah, distinctly I remember it was in the bleak December,
And each separate dying ember wrought its ghost upon the floor.
Eagerly I wished the morrow;—vainly I had sought to borrow
From my books surcease of sorrow—sorrow for the lost Lenore—
For the rare and radiant maiden whom the angels name Lenore—
> Nameless here for evermore.

And the silken sad uncertain rustling of each purple curtain
Thrilled me—filled me with fantastic terrors never felt before;
So that now, to still the beating of my heart, I stood repeating
" 'Tis some visitor entreating entrance at my chamber door—
Some late visitor entreating entrance at my chamber door;
> This it is and nothing more."

Presently my soul grew stronger; hesitating then no longer,
"Sir," said I, "or Madam, truly your forgiveness I implore;
But the fact is I was napping, and so gently you came rapping,
And so faintly you came tapping, tapping at my chamber door,
That I scarce was sure I heard you"—here I opened wide the door—
   Darkness there and nothing more.

Deep into that darkness peering, long I stood there wondering, fearing,
Doubting, dreaming dreams no mortals ever dared to dream before;
But the silence was unbroken, and the stillness gave no token,
And the only word there spoken was the whispered word, "Lenore?"
This I whispered, and an echo murmured back the word, "Lenore!"—
   Merely this and nothing more.

Back into the chamber turning, all my soul within me burning,
Soon again I heard a tapping something louder than before.
"Surely," said I, "surely that is something at my window lattice;
Let me see, then, what thereat is and this mystery explore—
Let my heart be still a moment and this mystery explore;—
   'Tis the wind and nothing more."

Open here I flung the shutter, when, with many a flirt and flutter,
In there stepped a stately Raven of the saintly days of yore.
Not the least obeisance made he; not a minute stopped or stayed he,
But, with mien of lord or lady, perched above my chamber door—
Perched upon a bust of Pallas just above my chamber door—
   Perched, and sat, and nothing more.

Then the ebony bird beguiling my sad fancy into smiling,
By the grave and stern decorum of the countenance it wore,
"Though thy crest be shorn and shaven, thou," I said, "art sure no craven,
Ghastly grim and ancient Raven wandering from the Nightly shore—
Tell me what thy lordly name is on the Night's Plutonian shore!"
   Quoth the Raven, "Nevermore."

SHEEP Party

✦✦✦✦✦

John Fuller

read by the poet

Under thorn and bramble
The sheep have left their rags
And decorate the valley
With little woollen flags.

"This way to the party,"
The wispy tufts declare,
"Between the banks and hedges,
Hurry, you're nearly there!

"There's bracken newly curling
And bilberry in bloom,
The guests are quite contented
And there's lots and lots of room."

But who am I to follow
And which way should I go?
The wool is blue and crimson
And from different sheep, I know.

The red-stained sheep live *that* way,
The blue-stained sheep up *there*.
There must be several parties
And I really couldn't care.

For I like peanut butter
Not grass and twigs and stones
Like the red sheep of Mr. Roberts
And the blue of Mr. Jones.

So why does Mr. Jones have blue sheep? In Great Britain, farmers often mark their sheep by painting their fleece a particular color to identify their flock.

66

JAMAICAN SONG

❖*❖*❖

James Berry

read by the poet

Little toad little toad mind yourself
mind yourself let me plant my corn
plant my corn to feed my horse
feed my horse to run my race—
the sea is full of more than I know
moon is bright like night time sun
night is dark like all eyes shut
    Mind—mind yu not harmed
    somody know bout yu
    somody know bout yu

Little toad little toad mind yourself
mind yourself let me build my house
build my house to be at home
be at home til one day vanish—
the sea is full of more than I know
moon is bright like night time sun
night is dark like all eyes shut
    Mind—mind yu not harmed
    somody know bout yu
    somody know bout yu

67

HALFWAY Down

❋ ❋

A. A. Milne

Halfway down the stairs
Is a stair
Where I sit.
There isn't any
Other stair
Quite like
It.
I'm not at the bottom,
I'm not at the top;
So this is the stair
Where
I always
Stop.

Halfway up the stairs
Isn't up,
And isn't down.
It isn't in the nursery,
It isn't in the town.
And all sorts of funny thoughts
Run round my head:
"It isn't really
Anywhere!
It's somewhere else
Instead!"

One chimpanzee.
Two crocodiles.
Three kings and a star made
Four... my new shoe size, just
Five days old. (I'm twice that now.) It's June—
Six more months until snow for sure.
Seven was lucky, not like
Eight, when I got glasses, better than
Nine, which felt Egyptian.

I'm ten now, which ends in
Zero. I've got
Four grandparents,
Three siblings,
Two parents and
One head with
Nothing to look at,
No place else to go.

Count To Ten And We'll Be There

❖❖❖

Rita Dove

read by the poet

Richard Wilbur

read by the poet

4 from *More Opposites*

What is the opposite of *pillow?*
The answer, child, is *armadillo.*
"Oh, don't talk nonsense!" you protest.
However, if you tried to rest
Your head upon the creature, you
Would find that what I say is true.
It isn't soft. From head to tail
It wears a scratchy coat of mail.
And furthermore, it won't hold still
Upon a bed, as pillows will,
But squirms, and jumps at every chance
To run away and eat some ants.

So there! Admit that I was right,
Or else we'll have a *pillow fight.*

7 from *More Opposites*

How often travelers who mean
To tell us some cave they've seen
Fall mute, forgetting how to use
Two dreadful words which they confuse!
The word *stalactite* is the first;
Stalagmite means the same, reversed.
Though both these things are formed in time
By dripping carbonate of lime,
Stalactites *hang*, while from beneath,
Stalagmites *rise* like lower teeth.

Can you remember that? You'll find
That you can fix those facts in mind
If you will frequently repeat,
While strolling down the village street
Or waiting for a bus to town,
"Stalagmites up! Stalactites down!"

Take care, though, not to be too loud,
Or you may draw a curious crowd.

20 from *Opposites*

What is the opposite of *hat?*
It isn't hard to answer that.
It's *shoes*, for shoes and hat together
Protect our two extremes from weather.

Between these two extremes there lies
A middle, which you would be wise
To clothe as well, or you'll be chilly
And run the risk of looking silly.

from

The Tale OF Custard the DRAGON

* * * * *

Belinda lived in a little white house,
With a little black kitten and a little gray mouse,
And a little yellow dog and a little red wagon,
And a realio, trulio, little pet dragon.

Now the name of the little black kitten was Ink,
And the little gray mouse, she called him Blink,
And the little yellow dog was sharp as Mustard,
But the dragon was a coward, and she called him Custard.

Custard the dragon had big sharp teeth,
And spikes on top of him and scales underneath,
Mouth like a fireplace, chimney for a nose,
And realio, trulio daggers on his toes.

Belinda was as brave as a barrel full of bears,
And Ink and Blink chased lions down the stairs,
Mustard was as brave as a tiger in a rage,
But Custard cried for a nice safe cage.

Belinda tickled him, she tickled him unmerciful,
Ink, Blink and Mustard, they rudely called him Percival,
They all sat laughing in the little red wagon
At the realio, trulio, cowardly dragon.

Belinda giggled till she shook the house,
and Blink said Weeck! which is giggling for a mouse.
Ink and Mustard rudely asked his age,
When Custard cried for a nice safe cage.

Good Hot DOGS

For Kiki

❋ ❋

Sandra Cisneros

Fifty cents apiece
To eat our lunch
We'd run
Straight from school
Instead of home
Two blocks
Then the store
That smelled like steam
You ordered
Because you had the money
Two hot dogs and two pops for here
Everything on the hot dogs
Except pickle lily
Dash those hot dogs
Into buns and splash on
All that good stuff
Yellow mustard and onions
And french fries piled on top all
Rolled up in a piece of wax
Paper for us to hold hot

In our hands
Quarters on the counter
Sit down
Good hot dogs
We'd eat
Fast till there was nothing left
But salt and poppy seeds even
The little burnt tips
Of french fries
We'd eat
You humming
And me swinging my legs

Lies, All Lies

William Cole

There is no ham in hamburger,
    And "allspice" is a cheat;
Applesauce is not a sauce,
    And sweetbreads aren't sweet.

There is no horse in horseradish—
    Why are we so misled?
There's no cheese in a headcheese,
    And sweetbreads aren't bread!

Ice cream on a stick,
Covered with cold, shiny chocolate,

Or ice cream heaped up in a cone,
Dripping fast on a hot day,

Or ice cream in a big blue bowl
And a spoon you can take your time with—

Which is the best?

It is too soon
To give the answer.

I have more testing
To do.

Which is the Best?

James Stevenson

75

Casey AT The Bat

❋ ❋ ❋

Ernest L. Thayer

performed by Poetry Alive!

The outlook wasn't brilliant for the Mudville nine that day;
The score stood four to two with but one inning more to play.
And then when Cooney died at first and Barrows did the same,
A pall-like silence fell upon the patrons of the game.

A straggling few got up to go in deep despair. The rest
Clung to the hope which springs eternal in the human breast;
They thought if only Casey could but get a whack at that—
We'd put up even money now with Casey at the bat.

But Flynn preceded Casey, as did also Jimmy Blake,
And the former was a hoodoo and the latter was a cake;
So upon that stricken multitude grim melancholy sat,
For there seemed but little chance of Casey getting to the bat.

But Flynn let drive a single, to the wonderment of all,
And Blake, the much despiséd, tore the cover off the ball;
And when the dust had lifted, and men saw what had occurred,
There was Jimmy safe at second and Flynn a-hugging third.

Then from five thousand throats and more there rose a lusty yell;
It rumbled through the valley, it rattled in the dell;
It pounded on the mountain and recoiled upon the flat,
For Casey, mighty Casey, was advancing to the bat.

There was ease in Casey's manner as he stepped into his place;
There was pride in Casey's bearing as a smile lit Casey's face.
And when, responding to the cheers, he lightly doffed his hat,
No stranger in the crowd could doubt 'twas Casey at the bat.

Ten thousand eyes were on him as he rubbed his hands with dirt;
Five thousand tongues applauded when he wiped them on his shirt.
Then while the writhing pitcher ground the ball into his hip,
Defiance flashed in Casey's eye, a sneer curled Casey's lip.

And now the leather-covered sphere came hurtling through the air,
And Casey stood a-watching it in haughty grandeur there.
Close by the sturdy batsman the ball unheeded sped—
"That ain't my style," said Casey. "Strike one," the umpire said.

From the benches, black with people, there went up a muffled roar,
Like the beating of the storm waves on a stern and distant shore.
"Kill him! Kill the umpire!" shouted someone on the stand;
And it's likely they'd have killed him had not Casey raised his hand.

With a smile of Christian charity great Casey's visage shone;
He stilled the rising tumult; he bade the game go on;
He signaled to the pitcher, and once more the dun sphere flew;
But Casey still ignored it, and umpire said, "Strike two."

"Fraud!" cried the maddened thousands, and echo answered,
        Fraud!"
But one scornful look from Casey and the audience was awed.
They saw his face grow stern and cold, they saw his muscles strain,
And they knew that Casey wouldn't let that ball go by again.

The sneer has fled from Casey's lip, his teeth are clenched in hate;
He pounds with cruel violence his bat upon the plate.
And now the pitcher holds the ball, and now he lets it go,
And now the air is shattered by the force of Casey's blow.

Oh, somewhere in this favored land the sun is shining bright;
The band is playing somewhere, and somewhere hearts are light,
And somewhere men are laughing, and little children shout;
But there is no joy in Mudville—mighty Casey has struck out.

The **Testing** TREE - part 1

*****

Stanley Kunitz

On my way home from school
            up tribal Providence Hill
                  past the Academy ballpark
where I could never hope to play
            I scuffed in the drainage ditch
                  among the sodden seethe of leaves
hunting for perfect stones
            rolled out of glacial time
                  into my pitcher's hand;
then sprinted lickety-
            split on my magic Keds
                  from a crouching start,
scarcely touching the ground
            with my flying skin
                  as I poured it on
for the prize of the mastery
            over that stretch of road,
                  with no one no where to deny
when I flung myself down
            that on the given course
                  I was the world's fastest human.

Skating
In the Wind

****

Kristine O'Connell George

I crouched.
My brother Bill shoved hard.
I held up my jacket;
the wind caught it, shaped it taut like a sail.

The wind slammed into my back.

My skates clattered.
Skidding,
Skimming,
like butter in a hot skillet.

Mouth dry,
the wind roared in my ears.

Bill said I was almost flying

Until the fence.

A Poem
for Jesse

your face like
summer lightning
gets caught in my voice
and i draw you up from
deep rivers
taste your face of a
thousand names
see you smile
a new season
hear your voice
a wild sea pausing in the wind.

❋ ❋

Sonia Sanchez

read by the poet

to P.J.
(2 yrs old who sed write a poem for me in Portland, Oregon)

if i cud ever write a
poem as beautiful as u
little 2/yr/old/brotha,
i wud laugh, jump, leap
up and touch the stars
cuz u be the poem i try for
each time i pick up a pen and paper.
u and Morani and Mungu
be our blue/blk/stars that
will shine on our lives and
makes us finally BE.
if i cud ever write a poem as beautiful
as u, little 2/yr/old/brotha,
poetry wud go out of bizness.

Chipmunks jump, and
Greensnakes slither.
Rather burst than
Not be with her.

Bluebirds fight, but
Bears are stronger.
We've got fifty
Years or longer.

Hoptoads hop, but
Hogs are fatter.
Nothing else but
Us can matter.

VALENTINE

❊ ❊ ❊

Donald Hall

SUMMER

W. D. Snodgrass

read by the poet

Summertime comes, and everyone takes wings,
But why catch planes when you could take a bird
And just land anyplace? Please take my word:
Birds give the smoothest ride since old porch swings
Or merry-go-rounds with music and brass rings.
No seatbelts, please, and it would be absurd
To put on earphones—everybody's heard
That for your listening pleasure, a bird sings.

All girls fly Western style now—not sidesaddle:
So pick a strong-winged mount with a tall crest
To skim across the prairies or skedaddle
Into a golden sunset in the West.
Then, when you're tired of galloping astraddle,
His wings and shoulders fold to form your nest.

When winds have their big pillow fights, the air
Fills up with stormy feather-swarms that keep
Piling themselves outdoors into a heap
High as your eyebrow. You can't get anywhere;
Why not just curl up in our Winter Chair
And snuggle down into a long, warm sleep
Protected by the overstuffed, soft, deep
Arms of comfy, star-marked Mother Bear?

What if you tried to go out for a stroll—
They'd stuff you into stiff snowsuits, socks, nubby
Sweaters, scarves, rubber boots till you'd look tubby
As any waddling, blubbed up, plump Bear Cub.
Your eyes keep oozing shut, so why not roll
Back into your own dark, star-sparked cubbyhole?

WINTER

read by the poet

83

The sun has a tail
that reaches under the earth
and tickles seeds.
That's what grandmother
once told me.
She says things grow
in laughter.

The Sun
HAS a TAIL

❖✳❖✳

Emanuel di Pasquale

Knoxville,
Tennessee

I always like summer
best
you can eat fresh corn
from daddy's garden
and okra
and greens
and cabbage
and lots of
barbecue
and buttermilk
and homemade ice cream
at the church picnic
and listen to
gospel music
outside
at the church
homecoming
and go to the mountains with
your grandmother
and go barefooted
and be warm
all the time
not only when you go to bed
and sleep

✳❖✳❖

Nikki
Giovanni

read by
the poet

TRACK 50

I am Cherry Alive

Delmore Schwartz

"I am cherry alive," the little girl sang,
"Each morning I am something new:
I am apple, I am plum, I am just as excited
As the boys who made the Hallowe'en bang:
I am tree, I am cat, I am blossom too:
When I like, if I like, I can be someone new,
Someone very old, a witch in a zoo:
I can be someone else whenever I think who,
And I want to be everything sometimes too:
And the peach has a pit and I know that too,
And I put it in along with everything
To make the grown-ups laugh whenever I sing:
And I sing: *It is true; It is untrue;*
I know, I know, the true is untrue,
The peach has a pit,
The pit has a peach:
And both may be wrong
When I sing my song,
But I don't tell the grown-ups: because it is sad,
And I want them to laugh just like I do
Because they grew up
And forgot what they knew
And they are sure
I will forget it some day too.
They are wrong. They are wrong.
When I sang my song, I knew, I knew!
I am red, I am gold,
I am green, I am blue,
I will always be me,
I will always be new!"

85

The Tyger

✶✶✶✶✶

William Blake

read by Elise Paschen

TYGER, tyger, burning bright
In the forests of the night,
What immortal hand or eye
Could frame thy fearful symmetry?

In what distant deeps or skies
Burnt the fire of thine eyes?
On what wings dare he aspire?
What the hand dare seize the fire?

And what shoulder and what art
Could twist the sinews of thy heart?
And when thy heart began to beat,
What dread hand and what dread feet?

What the hammer? what the chain?
In what furnace was thy brain?
What the anvil? What dread grasp
Dare its deadly terrors clasp?

When the stars threw down their spears,
And water'd heaven with their tears,
Did He smile His work to see?
Did He who made the lamb make thee?

Tyger, tyger, burning bright
In the forests of the night,
What immortal hand or eye
Dare frame thy fearful symmetry?

One day a mouse called to me from his curly nest:
"How do you sleep? I love curliness."

"Well, I like to be stretched out—I like the bones to be
All lined up. I like to see my toes way off over there."

"I suppose that's one way," he said, "but I don't like it.
The planets don't act that way—nor the Milky Way."

What could I say? You know you're near the end
Of the century when a sleepy mouse brings in the
  Milky Way.

Conversation
With
A MOUSE

* *

Robert Bly
read by the poet

"10 is a very important birthday.
It symbolizes the end of the single-number years."
—Billy Collins

On
Turning
TEN

❖ ❖ ❖

Billy Collins

read by the poet

The whole idea of it makes me feel
like I'm coming down with something,
something worse than any stomach ache
or the headaches I get from reading in bad light—
a kind of measles of the spirit,
a mumps of the psyche,
a disfiguring chicken pox of the soul.

You tell me it is too early to be looking back,
but that is because you have forgotten
the perfect simplicity of being one
and the beautiful complexity introduced by two.
But I can lie on my bed and remember every digit.
At four I was an Arabian wizard.
I could make myself invisible
by drinking a glass of milk a certain way.
At seven I was a soldier, at nine a prince.

But now I am mostly at the window
watching the late afternoon light.
Back then it never fell so solemnly
against the side of my tree house,
and my bicycle never leaned against the garage
as it does today,
all of the dark blue speed drained out of it.

This is the beginning of sadness, I say to myself,
as I walk through the universe in my sneakers.
It is time to say good-bye to my imaginary friends,
time to turn the first big number.

It seems only yesterday I used to believe
there was nothing under my skin but light.
If you cut me I would shine.
But now when I fall upon the sidewalks of life,
I skin my knees. I bleed.

X. J. Kennedy

read by the poet

How to Stay up LATE

At night when grown-ups start to yawn
Beneath their reading lamps
Is when I whip my album out
To stick in foreign stamps.

And when pajama time draws near
I start to write the story
Of Lincoln's life, or set up school
Like Maria Montessori.

So kids, wise up. Unless you like
To go to bed too fast
Just save your most impressive play
Of all day long for last.

Flashlight

Tucked tight in bed, the day all gone,
I like to click my flashlight on,
Then climb in under with my feet
And shine a moon out through the sheet.

I'll throw a circle on the wall,
Move close up to it, make it small,
And then yank back and make that moon
Blow up—an instant light-balloon!

Each flashlight battery, slid out,
Looks piglike with a silver snout
And like two pigs parading, they
Need to line up and look one way.

Ben Franklin with a kite and key
Attracted electricity,
But they must not be also-rans
Who put up light in little cans.

"Ever since I was a kid, I've been fascinated by flashlights.
They are powerful things to hold in your hand."
—X. J. Kennedy

Maturity

I take my plastic rocket ship
To bed, now that I'm older.
My wooly bear is packed away—
Why do the nights feel colder?

Wynken,
BLYNKEN,
and Nod

* ❋ *

Eugene Field

Wynken, Blynken, and Nod one night
  Sailed off in a wooden shoe, —
Sailed on a river of crystal light
  Into a sea of dew.
"Where are you going, and what do you
wish?"
  The old moon asked the three.
"We have come to fish for the herring fish
  That live in this beautiful sea;
  Nets of silver and gold have we!"
            Said Wynken,
            Blynken,
            And Nod.

The old moon laughed and sang a song,
  As they rocked in the wooden shoe;
And the wind that sped them all night long
  Ruffled the waves of dew.
The little stars were the herring fish
  That lived in that beautiful sea —
"Now cast your nets wherever you wish, —
  Never afeard are we!"
  So cried the stars to the fishermen three
            Wynken,
            Blynken,
            And Nod.

All night long their nets they threw
    To the stars in the twinkling foam, —
Then down from the skies came the wooden shoe,
    Bringing the fishermen home:
'Twas all so pretty a sail, it seemed
    As if it could not be;
And some folk thought 'twas a dream they'd dreamed
    Of sailing that beautiful sea;
    But I shall name you the fishermen three:
                Wynken,
                Blynken,
                And Nod.

Wynken and Blynken are two little eyes,
    And Nod is a little head,
And the wooden shoe that sailed the skies
    Is a wee one's trundle-bed;
So shut your eyes while Mother sings
    of wonderful sights that be,
And you shall see the beautiful things
    As you rock in the misty sea
    Where the old shoe rocked the fishermen three:—
                Wynken,
                Blynken,
                And Nod.

Two in Bed

* * *

Abram Bunn Ross

When my brother Tommy
Sleeps in bed with me,
He doubles up
And makes
himself
exactly
like
a
V

And 'cause the bed is not so wide,
A part of him is on my side.

I am the sister of him
And he is my brother.
He is too little for us
To talk to each other.

So every morning I show him
My doll and my book;
But every morning he still is
Too little to look.

Little

* * *

Dorothy Aldis

I had a little brother
And I brought him to my mother
And I said I want another
Little brother for a change.

But she said don't be a bother
So I took him to my father
And I said this little bother
Of a brother's very strange.

But he said one little brother
Is exactly like another
And every little brother
Misbehaves a bit, he said.

So I took the little bother
From my mother and my father
And I put the little bother
Of a brother back to bed.

In the audio, the poet explains that this
poem can be a tongue-twister.
How fast can you say it?

BROTHER

✤✤✤✤✤

Mary Ann Hoberman

read by the poet

The **Land** OF
Counterpane

❋❋❋❋

Robert Louis Stevenson

Counterpane means bedspread.

When I was sick and lay a-bed,
I had two pillows at my head,
And all my toys beside me lay
To keep me happy all the day.

And sometimes for an hour or so
I watched my leaden soldiers go,
With different uniforms and drills,
Among the bed-clothes, through the hills;

And sometimes sent my ships in fleets
All up and down among the sheets;
Or brought my trees and houses out,
And planted cities all about.

I was the giant great and still
That sits upon the pillow-hill,
And sees before him, dale and plain,
The pleasant Land of Counterpane.

These are the Beds
for me and for you!
These are the Beds
to climb into:

Pocket-sized Beds
and Beds for Snacks,
Tank Beds, Beds
on Elephant Backs,
Beds that fly,
or go under water,
Bouncy Beds, Beds
you can spatter and spotter,
Bird-Watching Beds,
Beds for Zero Weather—
any kind of Bed
as long as it's rather
special and queer
and full of surprises,

Beds of amazing
shapes and sizes—
NOT just a white little
tucked-in-tight little
nighty-night little
turn-out-the-light little
bed!

From **The Bed** BOOK

✦❖✦❖✦

Sylvia Plath

The **Coming**
OF
Teddy Bears

＊＊＊＊

Dennis Lee

The air is quiet
　　Round my bed.
The dark is drowsy
　　In my head.
The sky's forgetting
　　To be red,
And soon I'll be asleep.

A half a million
　　Miles away
The silver stars
　　Come out to play,
And comb their hair
　　And that's OK
And soon I'll be asleep.

And teams of fuzzy
    Teddy bears
Are stumping slowly
    Up the stairs
To rock me in
    Their rocking chairs
And soon I'll be asleep.

The night is shining
    Round my head.
The room is snuggled
    in my bed.
Tomorrow I'll be
    Big they said
And soon I'll be asleep.

Index

Acknowledgments

We are indebted to our insightful advisory editors, Billy Collins, Nikki Giovanni, and X. J. Kennedy, who each brought their unique spirit to the project. Thank you for lending your voices, poems, and knowledge. You provided the road map for this project and helped to steer it along the journey.

Many thanks to all the poets who contributed an abundance of inspiring work to the anthology and who also suggested their own childhood favorites. Your input was invaluable in crafting this introduction into the kaleidoscopic range that is poetry.

We were thrilled at the response from contemporary poets who enthusiastically lent their voices to the project. Whether it was the day after climbing a mountain or the day before traveling to France, these poets were ready to prove at a moment's notice that, indeed, poetry speaks. Thanks to the legions involved in making those recordings: Diana Gunnarson, Virginia Fowler, Tim Frantzich, Chuck Taylor, Paul Lancaster, Dunbar Wakayama, Bob Blank, Phil Kearney, Betty Smith at VPR, Daniel Kumin, Mount Holyoke Radio, Middlebury College Radio, Andy Haber, Joe Patty, Cara Kaifé Foster, Bob at Hagens video, and John and Laura Larsen at Larsen Recording, Chicago, Illinois. Special thanks to our friends in public radio and at NPR for the use of several of their studios and for their continual support of poets and poetry.

We also would like to express thanks to those who helped procure historical audio recordings. Don Glossinger, the Director of the Michigan City Public Library, was invaluable with his suggestions, relentless research and procuring of tapes—from the far reaches of New Zealand to his own audio archives. Thanks also to Don Varda at the Michigan City Public Library who helped convert and restore those recordings. We are much appreciative for the work of Karen Fishman, Jerry Hatfield, and Bryan Cornell at the Motion Picture, Broadcasting, and Recorded Sound Division of the Library of Congress, Richard Warren at Yale, Sam Hazo of the Spoken Page, and Annie Hughes at HarperAudio/Caedmon. We are indebted to Mike Konopka at Thundertone Audio for salvaging some archival tracks. And thanks to Andrew Medlar, Youth Material Specialist, at the Chicago Public Library, who first launched our audio quest.

Thanks to all those who introduce children to the lifelong love of poetry, especially librarians, teachers, and booksellers. Thank you to Claire Moore at Bookazine for assistance. Booksellers Liza Bernard and Penny McConnel from The Norwich Bookstore, Carol Chittenden from Eight Cousins, and Camille DeBoer from Pooh's Corner were helpful in the early stages of developing the book. A fond thanks to Becky Anderson of Anderson's Bookshops for her guidance.

Poetry Speaks to Children would not be the book it is without Christine Wilkinson of Wilkinson Studios and the gifted and tireless artists Judy Love, Wendy Rasmussen, and Paula Zinngrabe Wendland. Their unique styles evoke magic on each page.

Personal thanks to Stuart Brainerd, Bill Schmidt, and Ray Bennett for their continual support.

And, finally, immense gratitude to the staff at Sourcebooks: Todd Stocke for his quiet wisdom, know-how, and enduring calm, Samantha Raue for her astounding organizational skills and her ability to keep us always on track, the resourceful Jenn Frisbie, the intrepid Kay Mitchell, and the visionary designer Anne LoCascio, whose artistic eye and attention to detail show on every spread.

Contributors

EDITOR

Elise Paschen is the author of *Infidelities*, winner of the Nicholas Roerich Poetry Prize, and *Houses: Coasts*, and her poems have appeared in numerous magazines and anthologies. A graduate of Harvard University, she holds M.Phil. and D.Phil. degrees in twentieth century literature from Oxford University. Former Executive Director of the Poetry Society of America (1988–2001) and co-founder of "Poetry in Motion," a nationwide program that places poetry in subways and buses, she is the co-editor of *Poetry Speaks*, *Poetry in Motion*, and *Poetry in Motion from Coast to Coast*. Dr. Paschen teaches in the Writing Program at The School of the Art Institute of Chicago, and she lives in Chicago with her husband and their two children.

SERIES EDITOR

Dominique Raccah is founder, president, and publisher of Sourcebooks, a leading independent publisher outside of Chicago. Today Sourcebooks publishes nonfiction, fiction, and poetry. She is the series editor of *Poetry Speaks* and the Sourcebooks Shakespeare.

ADVISORY EDITORS

Billy Collins is the author of many volumes of poetry including *The Trouble with Poetry and Other Poems*, *Nine Horses*, *Sailing Alone Around the Room*, and *Picnic, Lightning*. His poems have appeared regularly in *The Best American Poetry*. He is a Distinguished Professor of English at Lehman College (City University of New York). He served as United States Poet Laureate (2001-03) and is currently the poet laureate of New York State.

A poet, lecturer, and educator, **Nikki Giovanni** has written more than two dozen books, including *Quilting the Black-Eyed Pea*, *Racism 101*, *Blues For All the Changes*, and *Love Poems*. *The Nikki Giovanni Poetry Collection*, a spoken-word CD, was a finalist for a Grammy Award in 2003. She is a three-time winner of the NAACP Image Award for Literature; she has also received the Langston Hughes award for Distinguished Contributions to Arts and Letters and The Rosa Parks Woman of Courage Award. She has been voted Woman of the Year by *Essence*, *Mademoiselle*, and *Ladies' Home Journal*. She is a University Distinguished Professor at Virginia Tech, where she teaches writing and literature.

X. J. Kennedy is the author of *Nude Descending a Staircase* (winner of the Lamont Award of the Academy of American Poets), *The Lords of Misrule*, which won the Poets' Prize, and other poetry books, as well as numerous works for children. With his wife, Dorothy, he edited *Knock at a Star: A Child's Introduction to Poetry*. Among his many awards is the National Council of Teachers of English Year 2000 Award for Excellence in Children's Poetry. Formerly the poetry editor of *The Paris Review*, Kennedy has taught at the University of Michigan, the Woman's College of the University of North Carolina, Wellesley College, the University of California–Irvine, the University of Leeds, and Tufts. Mr. Kennedy lives in Lexington, Massachusetts, with his wife.

ILLUSTRATORS

Judy Love says: "I currently live in a turn of the century house in Belmont, MA, with two cats, Fluffy and Jeremy, a parakeet called Tweed and a half dozen unnamed fish. I am very lucky to have two wonderful sons, Matt (21) and Tom (17), who are both accomplished artists. We enjoy going to museums and art shows together and whenever I need advice about one of my illustrations I can ask for their help. My life is full of art, music, theater, and friends. I can usually be found in my studio, perched on a high stool, drinking a huge mug of tea, listening to a book on tape and madly sketching while I try to keep Fluffy from walking all over my drawing. I've wanted to be an illustrator for as long as I can remember. Luckily I had parents that thought that this was a great idea, too. When I was eight years old my mother gave me a book of poetry with space around each verse to add a picture. Here I am almost fifty years later doing the same thing!"

Wendy Rasmussen has been drawing since the first time she could hold a crayon. She had a very creative father who told her stories and encouraged her to draw and inspired tales of trolls and other folklore. In fourth grade she wrote an essay called "Why I Want to Be an Illustrator When I Grow Up." An eye for detail comes from her love of science (she has a degree in Biology and a minor in Art) and her imaginative animals come from her father's fables. She lives in a remote area in Bucks County, Pennsylvania, where she is surrounded by wildlife that is a constant inspiration for her work. Her companions are two black labs and a cat, all of whom have served as models, whether they know it or not!

Paula Zinngrabe Wendland comes from a long line of artists; both of her parents are artists and her sister is a sculptor. She enjoys illustrating folk tales the most because her intense colors and stylized figures fit well with the imaginative tales. Her hobbies include figure skating, ceramics, designing crafts, and gardening. She has a redheaded husband, a daughter named Clara who is 12 years old and writes poetry, and a son, Nathan, age 9, who is a Jedi-wannabe and knows more about dinosaurs than anyone else Paula knows. She has a grumpy black cat named Schwartz.